PATTERNS IN NATURE

by Erin Ash Sullivan

Table of Contents

What Is a Pattern? . . . . .page 2

What Are Some Living Things
That Have a Pattern? .page 6

What Are Some Nonliving Things
That Have a Pattern? .page 12

What Is a Pattern?

A pattern is something that repeats over and over again.

Look at the pictures below. Can you find a pattern in each picture?

The chessboard has a pattern.
The light and dark boxes repeat over and over again.

The butterfly has a pattern, too.
Its yellow and black stripes repeat over and over again.

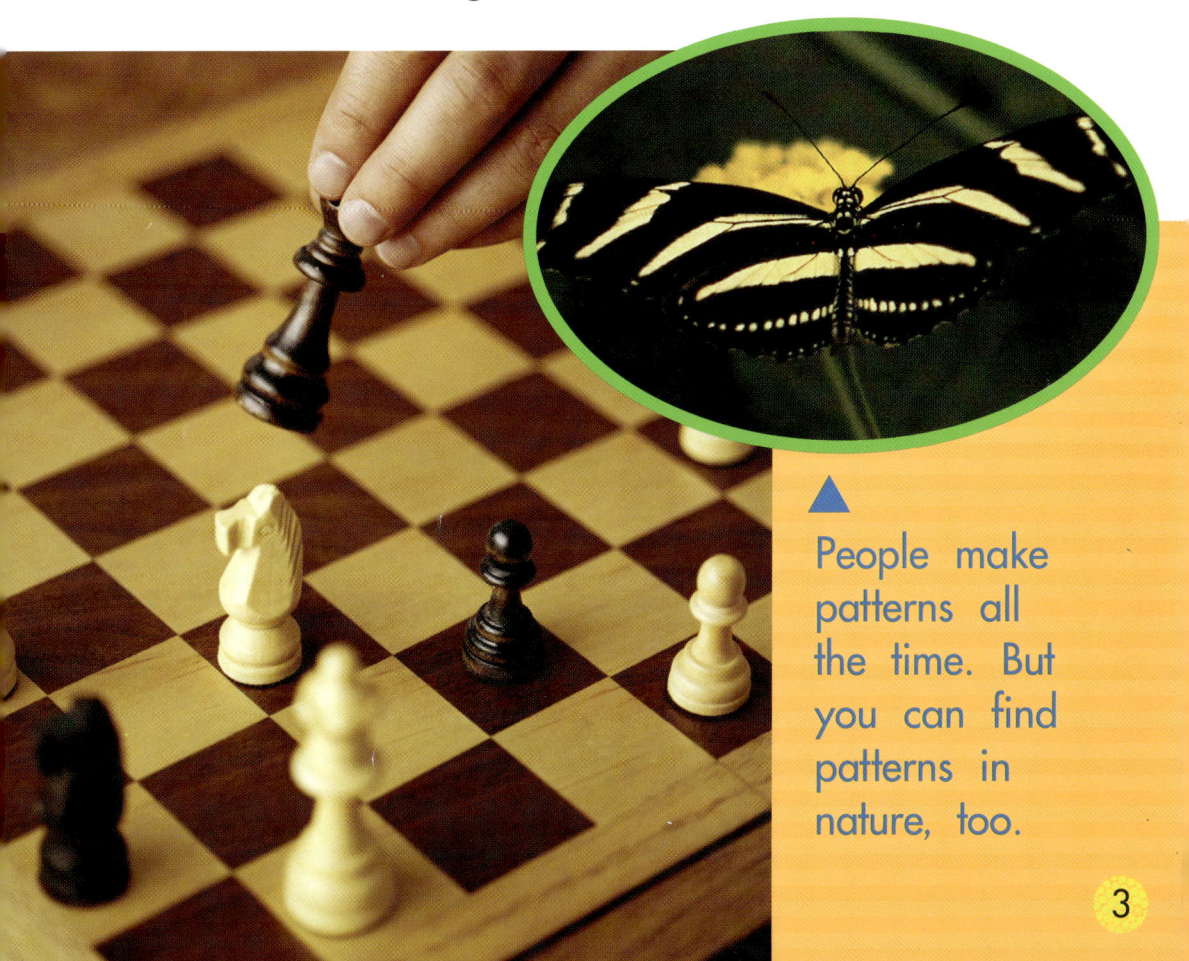

▲
People make patterns all the time. But you can find patterns in nature, too.

You can find patterns on many things in nature. You can find patterns on living things such as plants and animals.

Can you find a pattern on this flower?
▼

Can you find a pattern on this fish?
▼

4

You can find patterns on nonliving things, too. Honeycombs are nonliving things that have patterns.

▲ A honeycomb has a pattern of repeating shapes.

What Are Some Living Things That Have a Pattern?

Zebras have a pattern. The colors in their stripes repeat over and over again.

A zebra's pattern helps it hide in the tall grass.

▲ Look at the pattern on this zebra. Can you describe the pattern?

Many snakes have patterns.
Can you tell what the pattern is
on the snake in the picture?

Can you use the pattern to guess what comes next?

8

Many flowers have patterns, too. The colors yellow, red, yellow repeat on each of this flower's petals.

10

You can find patterns on trees. Tree trunks have a pattern of repeating rings.

Each ring of a tree trunk shows a year of the tree's life. You can use this pattern to tell how old a tree is.

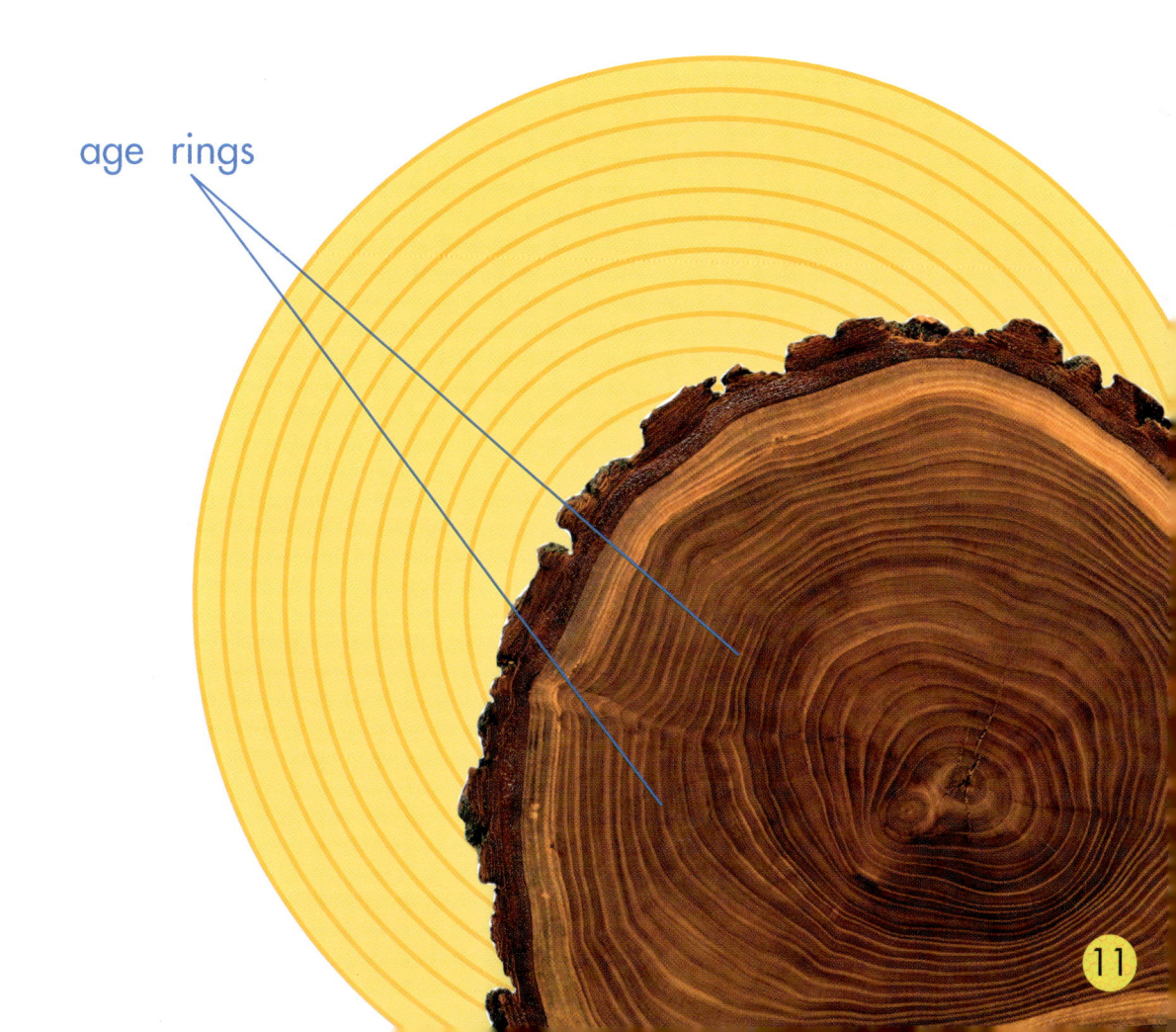

age rings

What Are Some Nonliving Things That Have a Pattern?

Rainbows are nonliving things that have a pattern. Every rainbow has the same pattern of colors.

Can you guess what comes next in this pattern?

A snowflake has a pattern. The shapes in a snowflake repeat over and over again.

Sometimes you can find a pattern in water, too. These water drops are making a pattern of repeating circles in the water.

If you look, you will find patterns everywhere in nature.